Do You
KNOW
Your
TEEN?

by Dan Carlinsky

SOURCEBOOKS, INC.
NAPERVILLE, ILLINOIS

Published by Sourcebooks, Inc.
P.O. Box 4410, Naperville, Illinois 60567-4410
(630) 961-3900
Fax: (630) 961-2168
www.sourcebooks.com

Library of Congress Cataloging-in-Publication Data
Dan Carlinsky
Do you know your teen? / by Dan Carlinsky.
p. cm.
ISBN 13: 978-1-4022-0681-8
ISBN 10: 1-4022-0681-X
Printed and bound in Canada
TR 10 9 8 7 6 5 4 3 2 1

If you're a parent, you probably think you know all about any kid of yours. Well—not so fast. Especially if that kid is a teenager, there are all sorts of things in your son's or daughter's life that you haven't a clue about. What does your teen really think about this or that? Really like and really loathe? What would your teen do in a given situation? How does your teen view friends, family, home, school, and the world?

This test challenges you with one hundred questions about that teen, some a little serious, some pure fun. Pick up a pen or pencil and give them your best shot. Then get your teen to sit down with you long enough to check your responses. Count ten points for each correct answer and rate your knowledge of that elusive specimen:

Above 900: Congratulations! How'd you do it?

800-900: A very fine performance. There's good communication going on.

600-790: Keep studying. You may improve before your teen hits 20.

Below 600: Well, no one ever really knows a teenager. That's part of their charm.

Good luck.

— D.C.

1. DO FRIENDS CALL YOUR TEEN BY A SPECIAL NICKNAME?
   _____ Yes: _____
   _____ No

2. IF YOUR TEEN COULD WATCH ONLY ONE TV SHOW A WEEK, WHICH WOULD IT BE?

   _____

3. DOES YOUR TEEN HAVE A FAVORITE COUSIN, AUNT, OR UNCLE?
   _____ Yes: _____
   _____ No

4. IF OFFERED A BIG SUM OF MONEY TO APPEAR IN A SOFT DRINK TV COMMERCIAL, WOULD YOUR TEEN:
   _____ Accept immediately?
   _____ Ask for time to think it over?
   _____ Say thanks but no thanks?

5. DOES YOUR TEEN HOPE TO GET MARRIED SOMEDAY? AT ABOUT WHAT AGE?
   _____ Yes, 20s
   _____ Yes, 30s or later
   _____ Maybe yes, maybe no
   _____ Never

6. YOUR TEEN'S POSITION ON FAST FOOD CHAINS:

_____ Likes some, won't set foot in _____

_____ Avoids them all

_____ Never met one that wouldn't do for three meals a day

7. IF A GENIE COULD MAKE IT HAPPEN OVERNIGHT, WOULD YOUR TEEN RATHER:

_____ Speak a foreign language fluently?

_____ Know how to pilot a plane?

_____ Be six inches taller?

8. THE LAST TIME YOUR TEEN BLEW BUBBLES WAS:

_____ Less than a year ago.

_____ A year or more ago.

_____ Too long ago to remember.

9. "ARE THERE MORE ADVANCED BEINGS ON OTHER PLANETS?" YOUR TEEN WILL SAY:

_____ "It's likely."

_____ "Could be."

_____ "No way."

_____ "Who cares?"

10. YOUR TEEN'S FAVORITE BOARD GAME OR PARTY GAME IS:

_____

11. FAVORITE VIDEO OR COMPUTER GAME?

_____

12. WHO AMONG YOUR TEEN'S FRIENDS AND ACQUAINTANCES IS THE BEST ARTIST?

_____

13. WHO'S THE TALLEST?

_____

14. AND WHO HAS THE MOST BROTHERS AND SISTERS?

_____

15. HOW WOULD YOUR TEEN RANK THESE ACTIVITIES, IN ORDER 1 TO 4?

_____ Hanging out at the mall
_____ Watching sports
_____ Playing sports
_____ Seeing a movie

16. AND THESE?

_____ Listening to a grandparent reminisce
_____ IMing with a schoolmate
_____ Running on a trail through the woods
_____ Browsing through a shelf of 19th-century books

17. IF ASKED TO PLAN A BEDROOM REDECORATION, YOUR TEEN WOULD CHOOSE _____ AS THE MAIN COLOR.

18. DOES YOUR TEEN HAVE A FAVORITE PHOTO OF HIM/HERSELF? WHICH ONE?

_____ Yes: _____

_____ No

19. CAN YOU NAME TWO NEWSPAPER COMIC STRIPS YOUR TEEN READS OFTEN?

_____

20. "WHERE DO GENERALS KEEP THEIR ARMIES? IN THEIR SLEEVIES." HOW WILL YOUR TEEN RATE THIS JOKE?

_____ A riot

_____ Corny but funny

_____ Corny and not funny

_____ Worst joke ever

21. A SCHOOL EXPERIMENT: DOING WITHOUT PHONE, TV, INTERNET, AND RECORDED MUSIC FOR A WEEK. YOUR TEEN WOULD FIND THE TEST:

_____ An interesting challenge

_____ Truly painful

_____ No big deal

22. CAN YOUR TEEN TIE A SQUARE KNOT?

_____ Yes, easily.

_____ Yes, with some effort.

_____ I think not.

23. WHICH WOULD YOUR TEEN CHOOSE FOR A NIGHT'S FUN?

_____ Watching an old-time movie comedy at a friend's house

_____ Attending a rock concert with a crowd

_____ Playing miniature golf with the family

24. DOES YOUR TEEN EVER TAKE NOTES IN CLASS AND THEN HAVE TROUBLE TROUBLE DECIPHERING THE HANDWRITING?

_____ All the time

_____ Occasionally

_____ Never

25. WHICH NEIGHBOR WOULD YOUR TEEN MOST LIKE TO SEE MOVE AWAY?

_____

26. "WHAT HOSPITAL WERE YOU BORN IN?" CAN YOUR TEEN ANSWER CORRECTLY?

_____ Yes

_____ No

27. HOW ABOUT THE NAME OF THE DOCTOR OR MIDWIFE WHO
    ASSISTED IN THE DELIVERY?

    _____ Yes
    _____ No

28. WHAT DO YOU REGULARLY DO THAT YOUR TEEN FINDS MOST
    EMBARRASSING?

    _____

29. IF GIVEN A CHOICE IN A CLASSROOM, YOUR TEEN USUALLY
    SITS:

    _____ In the front
    _____ In the back
    _____ In the middle

30. WHO WILL YOUR TEEN SAY IS THE YOUNGEST-ACTING OLD
    PERSON AROUND?

    _____

31. WHAT KIND OF DANCER WOULD YOUR TEEN CALL
    HIM/HERSELF?

    _____ Excellent
    _____ Good enough
    _____ The pits

32. YOUR TEEN ATTENDS AN EVENT AND WINS THE DOOR PRIZE: $100 TO ANY CHARITY. S/HE:

_____ Wants to give the money to _____.

_____ Asks around for suggestions about where to donate

_____ Complains about having to give up the cash

33. YOUR TEEN IS RIDING IN A CAR WITH A GROUP OF FRIENDS WHEN A TIRE BLOWS. NONE OF THE KIDS IS HURT, BUT SOMEONE HAS TO REMOVE THE FLAT TIRE AND INSTALL THE SPARE. YOUR TEEN:

_____ Takes over and does the job

_____ Tries to help some

_____ Sits nervously doing nothing

_____ Offers to phone for help

34. WHICH OF DOROTHY'S THREE FRIENDS FROM OZ CAN YOUR TEEN NAME?

_____ The Tin Man

_____ The Scarecrow

_____ The Cowardly Lion

35. WHAT'S YOUR TEEN'S FAVORITE HOLIDAY?

_____

36. WOULD YOUR TEEN SIGN A CARD DONATING BODY ORGANS FOR TRANSPLANT OR RESEARCH?

_____ Absolutely

_____ Maybe

_____ Never

37. DOES YOUR TEEN KNOW THE TYPICAL PRICE OF A QUART OF MILK?

_____ Yes

_____ No

38. CAN YOUR TEEN DO A HEADSTAND FOR AT LEAST 10 SECONDS?

_____ Yes

_____ No

39. YOUR TEEN THINKS THE DRINKING AGE IN YOUR AREA IS:

_____ Too low

_____ Too high

_____ Just right

40. A KILOMETER IS .625 MILES. DOES YOUR TEEN KNOW THAT?

_____ Yes

_____ No

41. DOES YOUR TEEN KNOW HIS/HER GRANDMOTHERS' MAIDEN NAMES?

_____ Yes

_____ No

42. WHAT ARTICLE OF CLOTHING DOES YOUR TEEN WISH YOU'D NEVER WEAR?

_____

43. DOES YOUR TEEN KNOW WHO PABLO PICASSO WAS?

_____ Yes

_____ No

44. HOW ABOUT HUMPHREY BOGART?

_____ Yes

_____ No

45. DOES YOUR TEEN KNOW THE COLOR OF A ROBIN'S EGG?

_____ Yes

_____ No

46. YOUR TEEN THINKS BURYING A DEAD PET CAT OR DOG WITH A HEADSTONE IS:

_____ Appropriate and sweet

_____ Demeaning to dead human beings

_____ No big deal—whatever people want

47. IF YOUR TEEN COULD PICK JUST ONE PIECE OF THE FAMILY
    FURNITURE TO KEEP FOREVER, IT WOULD BE:

    _____

48. IS THERE ONE COLOR M&M YOUR TEEN EATS FIRST OR
    SAVES FOR LAST?
    _____ First: _____
    _____ Last: _____
    _____ No special order

49. AT THE BEACH, YOUR TEEN PREFERS:
    _____ Sand
    _____ Rocks

50. IF GIVEN A CHOICE FOR A WEEKLONG HOLIDAY TRIP, YOUR
    TEEN WOULD SELECT:
    _____ Sailboat voyage
    _____ Bike tour
    _____ Safari

51. WHICH OF THESE MOVIE CATEGORIES IS YOUR TEEN'S
    FAVORITE?
    _____ Action
    _____ Romance
    _____ Comedy
    _____ Sci-Fi

52. WHAT MOVIE OR MOVIES HAS YOUR TEEN SEEN MORE THAN ONCE?

_____

53. WHAT WILL YOUR TEEN SAY IS THE BEST TV PROGRAM NO LONGER ON THE AIR?

_____

54. WHO'S YOUR TEEN'S FAVORITE TEACHER EVER?

_____

55. WHICH FRIEND DOES YOUR TEEN THINK HAS THE COOLEST PARENTS?

_____

56. WHICH FRIEND HAS THE MOST ANNOYING BROTHER OR SISTER?

_____

57. WHICH FAMILY MEMBERS DOES YOUR TEEN THINK S/HE RESEMBLES, EVEN A LITTLE?

_____

58. WHICH CELEBRITIES?

_____

59. WHEN WAS THE MOST RECENT TIME YOUR TEEN LOOKED UP AN UNFAMILIAR WORD IN A DICTIONARY (PRINT OR ONLINE)?

_____

60. IN THE PAST MONTH, HOW OFTEN HAS YOUR TEEN BORROWED OR LOANED SOMETHING (INCLUDING MONEY)?
Borrowed _____ times
Loaned _____ times

61. DOES YOUR TEEN KNOW WHO WON THE ACADEMY AWARDS FOR BEST ACTOR AND BEST ACTRESS MOST RECENTLY?
_____ Yes
_____ No

62. YOUR TEEN BELIEVES THAT:
_____ We have an immortal soul that survives the body.
_____ When we die, we die.

63. YOUR TEEN WOULD APPRECIATE A PRIVATE LESSON FROM AN EXPERT IN (CHOOSE AS MANY AS YOU THINK WILL FIT):
_____ Tennis
_____ Cooking
_____ Skydiving
_____ Tango
_____ Drawing, painting, or sculpting
_____ Photography
_____ Yoga

64. HAS YOUR TEEN EVER EATEN AN ENTIRE BOX OF COOKIES OR LARGE BAG OF CHIPS AT ONE SITTING?

_____ Often
_____ Once or twice
_____ Never

65. "CAN THERE BE SUCH A THING AS LOVE AT FIRST SIGHT?" YOUR TEEN WILL ANSWER:

_____ "I could fall in love at first sight."
_____ "Naw. It never really happens that way."
_____ "Can there be such a thing as love?"

66. WHO DOES YOUR TEEN CONSIDER THE FUNNIEST PROFESSIONAL COMEDIAN AROUND?

_____

67. AND WHO, AMONG FRIENDS, ACQUAINTANCES, AND RELATIVES OF ANY AGE, MAKES YOUR TEEN LAUGH MORE THAN ANY OTHER?

_____

68. IS THERE A PET OF YOUR TEEN'S DREAMS?

_____ Yes: a _____
_____ No

69. WHICH OF THESE WOULD YOUR TEEN NEVER CONSIDER AS A PET?

_____ Lizard

_____ Rabbit

_____ Fish

_____ Bird

_____ Ferret

70. WHICH OF THESE MUSIC TYPES WILL YOUR TEEN LISTEN TO WITHOUT COMPLAINT?

_____ Rap

_____ Rock

_____ Country

_____ Christian

_____ Jazz

_____ Classical

71. NAME AT LEAST TWO OF YOUR TEEN'S FAVORITE BANDS OR SINGERS.

_____

72. WHAT CURRENT BAND, SINGER, OR SONG DOES YOUR TEEN ABSOLUTELY LOATHE?

_____

73. CAN YOU MATCH YOUR TEEN'S PICKS?

_____ Summer   or   _____ Winter
_____ Horses   or   _____ Cows
_____ Morning   or   _____ Night

74. THREE MORE:

_____ Red   or   _____ Orange
_____ Pizza   or   _____ Tacos
_____ Eating   or   _____ Sleeping

75. THE HOUSE OF YOUR TEEN'S DREAMS WOULD HAVE:

_____ A huge in-ground swimming pool
_____ A fully equipped home theater
_____ A spectacular professional kitchen

76. YOUR TEEN'S DREAM CAREER:

_____

77. YOUR TEEN THINKS KIDS WHO WRITE POETRY ARE PROBABLY:

_____ Interesting
_____ Pretentious
_____ Smart
_____ Weird

78. YOUR TEEN'S FAVORITE ICE CREAM FLAVOR IS:

_____

79. WOULD YOUR TEEN PREFER TO:
_____ Eat three meals a day?
_____ Eat twice a day?
_____ Eat just one big meal a day?
_____ Graze all day and night?

80. HAS YOUR TEEN EVER MADE UP A LANGUAGE OR USED A
SECRET HANDSHAKE OR SIGN WITH A FRIEND OR SIBLING?
_____ Yes
_____ No

81. WHICH CHILDHOOD CARTOON
CHARACTER DOES YOUR
TEEN REMEMBER MOST
FONDLY?

_____

82. WOULD YOUR TEEN RATHER
GROW UP TO BE:
_____ Fantastically rich but
with no real friends?
_____ Barely scraping by but
with zillions of friends?

83. YOUR TEEN:

_____ Has always liked his/her name

_____ Once disliked it but likes it now

_____ Would change it to _____

84. WHICH OF THESE LABELS WOULD YOUR TEEN APPLY TO HIM/HERSELF?

_____ Moody

_____ Stubborn

_____ Understanding

_____ Shy

_____ Hardworking

_____ Open-minded

_____ Insecure

_____ Reliable

_____ Nerdy

_____ Talkative

85. WHAT STATION IS YOUR TEEN'S RADIO MOST OFTEN TUNED TO?

_____

86. THIS WEEKEND, YOUR TEEN WOULD LOVE TO:

_____ Bungee jump

_____ Go to a concert

_____ Ride on a fire truck

_____ Adopt a puppy

87. WHAT FAMOUS PERSON WOULD YOUR TEEN MOST LIKE TO MEET?

_____

88. WHERE WILL YOUR TEEN SAY S/HE LEARNS MOST ABOUT WHAT'S GOING ON IN THE WORLD?

_____ Newspaper

_____ Magazine

_____ Radio

_____ TV

_____ Internet

_____ People talking

89. IS THERE A STORE THAT OTHER KIDS SHOP IN THAT YOUR TEEN DETESTS?

_____ Yes: _____

_____ No

90. COULD YOUR TEEN IDENTIFY HIS/HER BEST FRIEND JUST BY LOOKING AT THE FRIEND'S FEET?

_____ Yes, the shoes would give it away.

_____ No, there'd be no way to tell.

91. IS YOUR TEEN A NOTEBOOK DOODLER?

_____ Yes—on almost every page

_____ Now and then

_____ No doodles at all

92. YOUR TEEN THINKS STAR SCHOOL ATHLETES:

_____ Are usually hardworking and deserve public praise

_____ Get too much attention

93. OF THESE, THE PROFESSION YOUR TEEN HAS THE MOST RESPECT FOR IS:

_____ Teacher

_____ Clergyman

_____ Reporter

_____ Medical doctor

_____ Small-business owner

_____ Big-company CEO

_____ Carpenter

94. IN WHICH OF THESE CATEGORIES DOES YOUR TEEN KNOW AT LEAST ONE KID FOR CONVERSATION BEYOND "HI"?

_____ Jock

_____ Intellectual

_____ Gay

_____ Super-popular

_____ Computer freak

95. IF YOU ASK YOUR TEEN TO THINK OF SOMEONE WHO HAS A MUSTACHE, S/HE'LL SAY:

" _____ "

96. AND IF YOU SAY, "NAME A BALD MAN," YOUR TEEN WILL RESPOND:

" _____ "

97. HAS YOUR TEEN EVER BEEN CAUGHT SLEEPING IN CLASS? (TEN BONUS POINTS IF YOU KNOW THE TEACHER.)

_____ Yes, in _____ 's class

_____ No

98. DOES YOUR TEEN KNOW THE FIRST NAME OF EACH OF HIS/HER CURRENT TEACHERS?

_____ Yes, all of them

_____ Some

_____ None

99. WOULD YOUR TEEN LIKE TO GET AN ULTIMATE MAKEOVER?

_____ Yes

_____ No

100. WOULD YOUR TEEN LIKE *YOU* TO GET ONE?

_____ Yes

_____ No